Her Wilde *Heart*

Dear Michelle ~
I'm so glad
Her Wilde Heart
found a great home!
Enjoy! Artemis

ARTEMIS SKYE MCNEIL

Her Wilde Heart
Copyright © 2018 by Artemis Skye McNeil

Library of Congress Control Number: 2018932017
ISBN-13:   Paperback: 978-1-64151-446-0
              PDF: 978-1-64151-447-7
              ePub: 978-1-64151-448-4
              Kindle: 978-1-64151-448-4

Printed in the United States of America

LitFire LLC
1-800-511-9787
www.litfirepublishing.com
order@litfirepublishing.com

CONTENTS

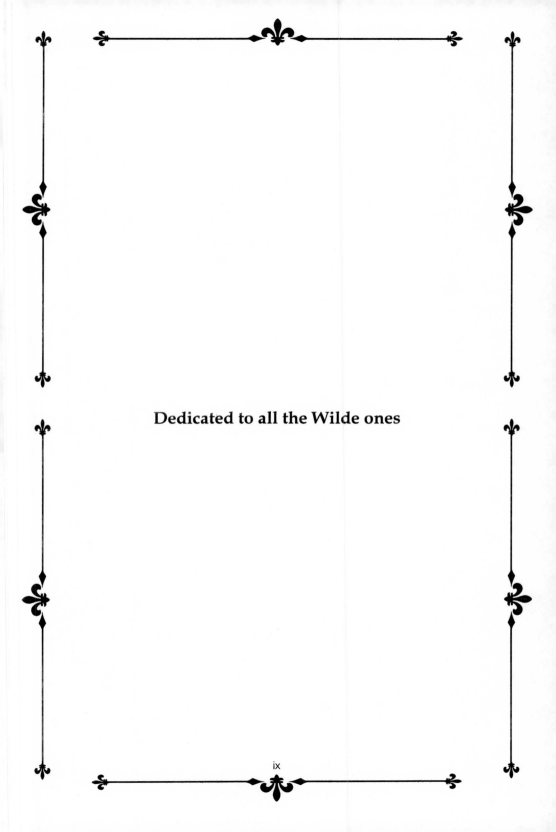

Dedicated to all the Wilde ones

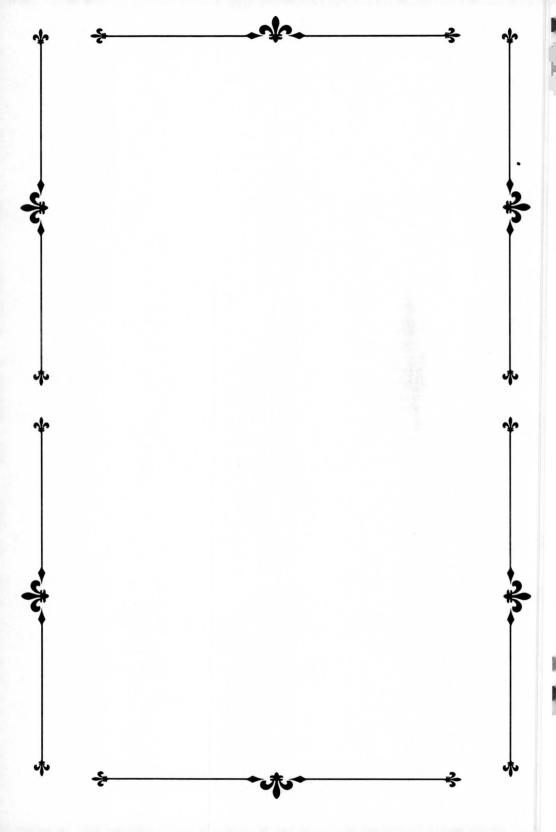

INTRODUCTION

*"We are artists and poets. We are
everyday people. We are crowds and
loneliness wrapped up in one soul."*
-Artemis

"Her (Oscar) Wilde Heart" is for those with art and poetry scrawled in their heart and a wry sense of humor embedded in their soul. It's for the multi-faceted, diverse outside-the-box thinkers, who are simply and beautifully complicated.

It calls to those who believe that *"Everything is art"* and that *"Nothing is ordinary when it is loved."*

It is for the witty, forever hopeful romantics, and those who fight for the right to play, dream, and create, while pretending to be grown.

This is a complement to all the people we are on the inside.

Interspersed with quotes from Oscar Wilde, past and present intermingle seamlessly, showing that poetry, life's observations, and human nature is timeless.

"Her Wilde Heart" is not a typical poetry book.

It's not one you curl up on the couch with a nice cup of tea and read from cover to cover (although you certainly can if you want to).

This is an interactive book. Throw it in your bag or briefcase. Carry it with you.

Grab it time and again to reignite your fire, for laughter, for a quiet moment snuck away, or a good swift kick in reality's butt.

Divided into three sections:

1. Works of Art(emis) - The Romances
2. Poetry Flows Through Life: Inspirational Quotes
3. Cheeky Stuff - The Lightning Round

Your part:

Separate the sections with book markers, heck, dog ear the pages if you want.

Read it aloud, mark in it, write your own poetry in the margins, jot down thoughts when inspired, or add your own additional commentary to what's already there. So, whether you're in the mood for classic poetry, searching for inspiration, seeking inner reflection to help you get through a moment, or looking for a little bit of sarcastic humor, let this be a go-to book for all the different people you are during the course of the day (week, month, year after year).

"I needed a place to hide my secrets,
so I became a writer."
    -Artemis

A Taste of Art

(Try Me Page)

"Works of Art(emis)"

The Romances

I Will Love You

I will love you to the end of your crooked smile,
through the tracks of your fallen tears,
between the cracks of your broken heart.
I will love you while the chips are down
and the stakes are high.
I will stick by your side
as assuredly as you have stuck by mine;
when you made me smile,
wiped my tears,
healed my heart.
I will love you as you've loved me,
then I will add some love on top
just to sweeten the deal a bit more.
I will love you.
Yes, I will.

Poetry Flows Through Life:
Inspirational Quotes

Unstoppable

You cannot drown what lives in the deep
nor set fire to what already burns.

Be relentless
Hands cannot choke a soul.
A fire burning in the bones
can never be extinguished.

Cheeky Stuff:
The Lightning Round

Tongue-in-cheek wit and good-natured humor

Universal Negotiator

They say you can speak it into existence.
Now I'm in full blown negotiations with the universe.

I hope you enjoyed the appetizer. Get ready to dig in.

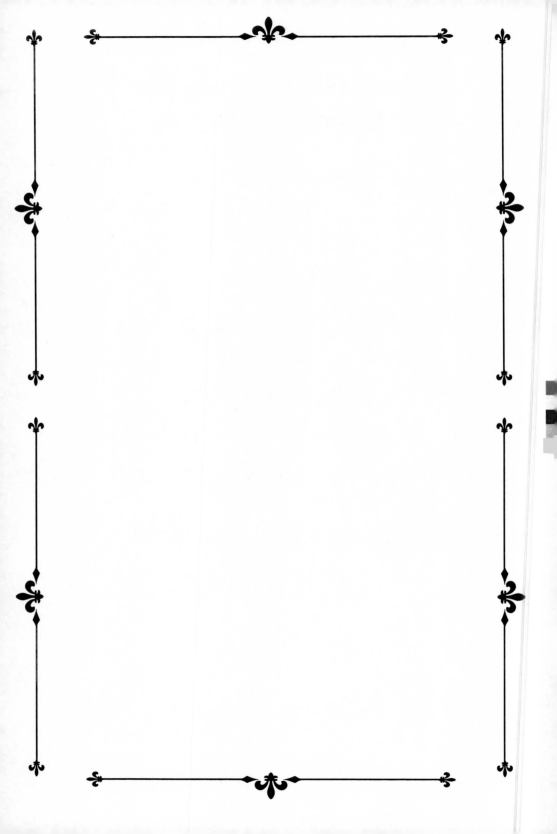

SECTION 1

Works of Art: The Romances

*"Keep love in your heart. A life without it is like
a sunless garden when the flowers are dead."*
               -Oscar Wilde

I Believe

I love how you see me as all I can be,
and make me believe I already am.

Then there's LOVE

It's not like I didn't live, or love, or laugh before I met you.
It's more like I didn't LIVE, or LOVE,
or LAUGH before I met you.

That's exactly what it was like.

One and a Million

I would choose you a million times over,
but I'm glad I had the chance, even once.

Renewed

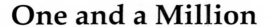

We laugh and play and love each other.
More importantly, we save each other a little
everyday without even trying.

Accountability

I am holding you personally accountable
for making me fall in love with you, and absolutely
responsible for all the kisses you are about to receive.

The Perfect "Complicationship"

We're such a lovely paradox you and I.

In a perfect complicationship.

Nothing and Everything

It was eating cereal in bed laughing
at Saturday morning cartoons.
It was lazy Sundays strolling hand in hand
under new and harvest moons.
It was you placing Star Jasmine in my hair.
It was driving through winding roads,
while Stevie Ray filled the air.
It was quiet reading, and crossword puzzles
while our legs were intertwined,
to a background of lazy blues.
It was nothing special yet it was everything magical,
because it was doing nothing yet everything, with you.

Her Oscar Wilde Heart

The city that never sleeps plays in her eyes.
They dance and sparkle in hope.
Her Oscar Wilde heart
assures she won't be understood,
so don't try.
But, don't pass her by,
you'd only be denying yourself.
Stay in her town, rest a while.
Refresh yourself in her warmth.
Exhilarate yourself with her mind.
You'll be the better one for having found her
even when she wasn't looking for you,
but she took you in. That means something.

Love her,
yes love her fiercely,
because her spirit is generous
and her soul is welcoming and willing.
She will make you feel things you've never felt.
She will make you feel you belong,
like you found your way home,
even if only a temporary squatter
passing through her heart.

And after you're long gone,
your thoughts will travel back to her in
sleepless visions and untamed dreams.
The hum of your own heart forever changed.
She can hear it, for wherever you roam,
you now remain her affectionate friend.

For those who love deeply, poetically, creatively.
For those who dream.
For those forever misunderstood, which is
not always an unwelcome title.
For those forever elusive
so that they can't explain you,
yet they know you are a unique and special breed.

I Will Love You

I will love you to the end of your crooked smile,
through the tracks of your fallen tears,
between the cracks of your broken heart.
I will love you while the chips are down
and the stakes are high.
I will stick by your side
as assuredly as you have stuck by mine;
when you made me smile,
wiped my tears,
healed my heart.
I will love you as you've loved me,
then I will add some love on top
just to sweeten the deal a bit more.
I will love you.
Yes, I will.

To love and be loved back through thick and thin is a special thing.

Stoked

Kindle your bones piece by piece.
Stoke the verve in your spirit that I so admire.
Let your soul find breath and release,
and set your heart on fire.

Heated

He felt the fire in me and drew closer.
He wasn't afraid of the heat.
He said his soul hadn't felt
the warmth of a true flame for the longest time.
I promised he'd never be cold or alone again.

In every quiet thought there is a raging fire.

Bated

The mist of silent fog forms beyond a
window of distant wonder.
Bated breath of desire swirls forming glass into canvas.
The drawing of diaphanous hearts with calculated finger
takes away the permanence of that which is written on walls,
so we proceed without reticence,
throwing caution a curve ball.
We stare out into the stark cold warming each other.
Our contrasts play well together.
Kindred spirits fueling fantasy with unceasing imagination.
The goose bumps on your skin are telling
of what we both secretly wish.
Hushed ambitions are no inhibitor to dream overload,
for in every quiet thought is a raging fire.

From romance to life goals, we constantly seek personal fulfillment.
Hushed ambitions.
Dream overload.
In every quiet thought there is a raging fire.

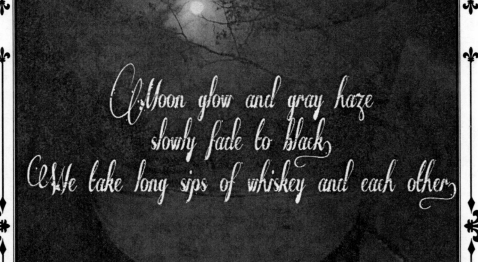

Moon glow and gray haze
slowly fade to black,
We take long sips of whiskey and each other

Moon Glow and Whiskey Haze

Moon glow and gray haze slowly fade to black.
We take longs sips of whiskey
and each other.
Stealing moments,
freezing time,
etching memoirs
with shadows on silent walls-
Lost in our own abandoned world.

Just Three Things

I can use a drink,
a love song,
and you.

They Resurface

I find it quite the irony
picking up a bottle
to drink your memory down.
You see, bottled up thoughts
of you simply don't drown.

I buried your
memories
down deep
in order to forget you.
Now I find you
rooted in my soul.

Rooted

I buried your memories down deep
in order to forget you.
Now I find you rooted
in my soul.

Again I fall for you
like dominoes

Although weightless
when you're near.

Love's contradictions are far too clear.

The Fall and Rise

Again my chest falls and rises in quickened breath
while feeling I cannot catch it at all.
Yet, with the warmth of yours at my neck -
I am saved.
Indeed, the heart declares love's contradictions
with gleeful irony and sheer abandon.

Still

Cursed circumstance that arrests my breath.
-Arms slacken
Thighs tighten as steel-
This ribcage cannot contain the
beating mayhem that runs off
with my common sense.
It wreaks havoc through this
helpless body with every glimpse,
thought, and trace of you.
Alas, my vessel receives no remedy for reprieve
-still

Intrinsic

In the by and by
hand's fate may crimp mine own
to slacken dexterity and desire for printed page.

Perhaps pen strokes
of a by gone era meet with
perusal's neglect
for the dimmed light of mine eye.

Then too may fractured memory
rise up as enemy
seeking my cognizant demise.
Once beautiful memories of reminiscence
violated to mere tumbleweed blowing
through a broken mind.

However, aimed the arrows
to this poet's Achilles' Heel,
one vital truth shall remain
constant and rule
victorious over ill winds.

The soul fated veracity
that I once called you mine
lives indestructible.
This kindred intrinsic,
an insulated treasure carried
in my bosom.

Prodigious love sewn by destiny,
bound by more than stars.
Attempts to wrench you
from my "marrowed bone"
will be met with sheer displeasure.
From erstwhile to eternal,
our hearts embedded in one another,
for the markings have been made
through and through.

Biology

I laugh as he studies my freckles intensely.
I tell him there's no pop quiz
on how many there are.
But secretly, I don't mind being
his homework assignment one bit.

XOXO

Of all the letters in the alphabet
I have at my disposal
to describe love,
my favorite ones are X's and O's
when it comes to you.

Round Trip Dreams

Thoughts of running
from all the fakeness in this world
were always one way,
until you.
Now I have a round trip ticket
with dreams of coming home
to something true.

Behind My Back

You climbed my spine like a tingle,
adeptly working your way through guarded ribs.
Then right behind my back, you absconded with my heart.

Litto Heart Thief

You stole my heart.
Everything else I hand over to you freely.

Wrecked

You've got me heart wrecked and mind totaled.
But this is no accident.
You know how to shift your love into overdrive
and send me drifting.

Night Light

Let the sky conceal hope's stars.
Tonight I wish upon the darkness
in your arms.

Sometimes the light is found in the dark.

Captured Pt 1

Relinquish your heart!
Surrender!
Your love is under siege by my weapons
of ultimate romance and subterfuge of passion.
I render you powerless under the ardor of my spell,
carrying you off as willing prisoner.
Feign protest, if you must.
But, you know with avidity
that you are solely and forever mine
(I've been captured by you too).

Captured Pt 2

When her voice lingers on your skin,
when being captivated by her eyes
becomes a voluntary prison,
when loving her sets you free;
then plead guilty.
Let her arrest your heart
-willing to remain captured.

DNA Deep

I won't stop digging until I have your soul
under my nails and your heart between my teeth.
There is no recourse, but to reveal your true self-
The secret person you protect will be *exposed*
-'cause I'm going DNA deep.
All masks asunder, naked truth be confessed;
until I feel pure honesty, there will be no rest.

My Living Diary

You are my bound love whom I confess to
for you read me without judgement.
I pour out to you in ink's blood
bliss and tears,
magical moments and tragedy,
failure and success,
strengths and flaws.
My every secret is kept in you-
and you regard them all as treasure.
In your spine you carry my stories.
Inside your covers I become poetry.
Your are the place I found to lay my words.
You are my living diary.

Are we not all poetry in search for a place to lay down our words?

Spinal Column

My spine contains endless raveled tales;
past stories indelibly written on bone and sinew.
Words pulsate like an encumbered heart
breathing off the page;
wounded words
bellicose words
defeated words
hopeful words
The story continues-
A new chapter begins and there you are.
You cover me with your love and
smooth out the creases of my dog-eared soul
under gentle fingers.
You peruse all that I am with your eyes.
All my narrative exposed-
I have become an open book in your hands.
I confess I wish to skip ahead,
eager to read our happy ending.

Eternal Light

Even if the gleam
should dim from my eye,
my heart would remain ablaze for the fire
you've kindled in my every bone.
Marrow deep, scintillating embers
stoked so that my very ash would illuminate
at the last passing thought of you.
This, the eternal light your love
has gifted me.

You, My Eternity

YOU
MY ultimate destiny.
We may have lost years,
but our love will go down in history.
These moments between us, an ETERNITY.

Measuring Eternity

We were eternal,
for we measured our love
in smiles, not years.

Just One More Day

I will love you for eternity,
then ask for one more day.

That's a Wrap

I wrap around you like paper,
for you are my rock.

*No scissors required,
'cause I will never cut you
out of my life*

Hushed

She is his unburdening,
a soft voice on the wind that carries him through.

Secret Smile

You are the reason I secretly smile,
randomly and often.
Like a shared inside joke,
I catch myself daydreaming and laughing
just a little too much.

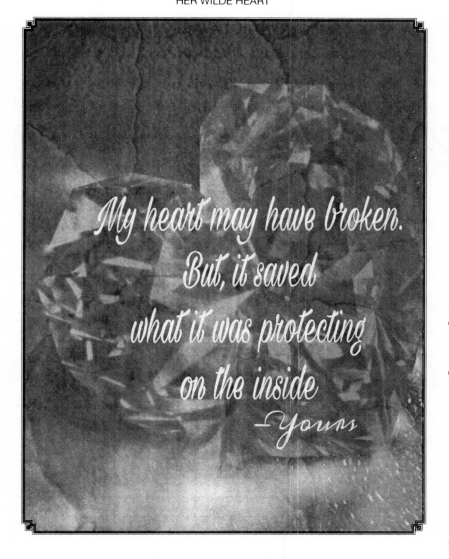

My heart may have broken.
But, it saved
what it was protecting
on the inside
—Yours

The Sacrifice

My heart may have broken, but it saved
what it was protecting on the inside
-yours.

*"Some things are more precious,
because they don't last long."
-Oscar Wilde*

A Distant Light

I love you even now, though far from me.
I imagine how your smile lights up a distant room,
how the energy of your presence brings others joy.
And I smile at how deeply your distant
light can still make me all aglow.

Twilight's Ache

I think of you during the day,
what you might be up to,
what you might say,
how your smile entices,
how your sparkling eyes play.
Under the moonlight
I dance with your ghost.
With slow, sultry moves
we sway back and forth.
Exchanging wine flavored kisses,
in fantasies I'm lost.
But in the twilight,
in the early hours of light's first stream,
I ache for you like crazy,
reaching out longingly to draw you
into these empty arms
as you slowly vanish from my dreams.

"I Miss You"

Last night in my dreams emerged the words,
"I miss you," dancing like diaphanous ribbon
on a background of black infinite.

Was I the intended recipient of this ethereal note,
or the subconscious sender?

An enigmatic message that hovered in darkness.

Soporific butterflies fluttered, hesitation ensued.
Through drowsy mind a tickling stupor of question.

One thing was guaranteed, the betrothed message
of longing was exclusive.
It belonged to none other than us.
A thought, I cannot shake in sleep or wake,
of this I am certain.
Even when bright eyed and bushy tailed,
I still utter the dreamy words.
Wide awake, from me to you,
"I miss you darling, I do."
I really do.

Leased Hearts

Let's not fool ourselves into believing we own another.
We do not control hearts.
If by some fortune
we stumble upon a heart that seeks ours,
we randomly and loosely steer each other for a time.
Voluntary surrender
with an accompanied smile.
That is the loveliest we should ever wish to enjoy.

NO POINT...period!

You say you need time...
Even though I will respect your request,
question marks swirl in my head,
and I pray this is only a comma
separating our love and not a period,
because I will never see the point for the space between us!

*No period, out of protest, because there is no point
to you having left...*

"New Normal"

Of course, you won't die after I'm gone.
You'll live.
But it won't be the same.
It will never be the same.
You'll be changed forever for having known me.
It will be your "new normal."

Undone

You cannot unremember the warmth of my arms,
unfeel my burning kisses from your eager lips,
unhear my name playing through your mind
that you called out so often.
The only thing undone is you.
Because, you my darling,
will never unmemory me.

So Untry

Eye Escape

I may still be captivated by your eyes;
but I am no long a prisoner of your charms.

Almost

We were a near death experience.

Small Victories

I almost cried over you today
-*almost*.
Here's to small victories.

Confessions: Forgetting You

When the poems about forgetting you stop,
then it will be true.

How can I write about forgetting you and not remember?

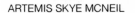

Paper Hearts and Those of Stone

Oh splintered heart!
My next one shall be made of paper
to cover your rock like one.
Then I shall win.

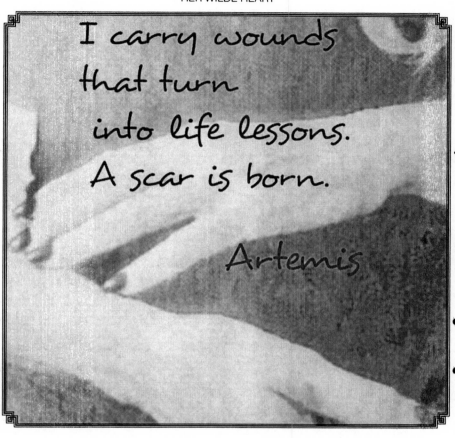

I carry wounds
that turn
into life lessons.
A scar is born.

Artemis

Scars Mean Victory

As I touched a faint scar on my arm from a childhood injury,
I remembered running into my mother's arms crying
after falling and scraping myself.
Her soft voice and warm hug soothed me.
She promised that one day it wouldn't hurt anymore.
At that moment, I realized that with you in my life my love,
my heart too, would soon heal.

Comforting words and soothing touches are healers.

43

I Hum You Back To Me

The music died a while back.
But if I hum the poetry you left behind, I can
still feel the rhythm of the love we shared
that keeps me alive.

Memory

In memory you still teach me.
Even the ghost of you is stronger than
flesh and blood that surrounds me.

Sometimes our most present and persistent teachers,
are those from the past.

Never Forgotten

We sprightly raise the chalice and soberly lower the boom.
In extant celebrations of life we partake,
and mourn the light of those extinguished too soon.

"The curves of your lips rewrite history."
-Oscar Wilde

The She Files (lol)

She's cute,
with just enough crazy
to keep it interesting.

Wild My Tame

You set fire to all that burns in me.
You create welcome chaos and bliss.
You bring meaning to my sentences,
with a child's laughter and vixen's kiss.
You're the one I can't refuse,
the ache for all I miss.

You are the variable and the constant,
the different and the same.
You're the only who tames my restlessness
and unabashedly wilds my tame.

A Force of Nature

She's not the type of storm you take shelter from.
She's the downpour you get drenched in, the rain
you get soaked to the skin for,
overcome by the flashes of her lightning
and the rhythm of her thunder.

Body of Work

It was the elegant curve at the nape of her neck,
her undulating signature of a walk, and those
inspiring contours for hips that finished the lines
to his poem.

Statuesque

Please don't place me on a pedestal.
It's a base for lifeless statues
and vulnerable to bird droppings.

I want to be right by your side.

Mona Lisa

She is art and beauty in the making.
What was the Mona Lisa,
but passionate brushstrokes of love
birthing a Masterpiece to life?

The Morphing of a Real Woman

Just when you think she's earthy,
she's sexy.
Just when you think she's sexy,
she blindsides you with the facts.
Just when you think she's an intellect,
she whimpers in childlike innocence.
Just when you think she's vulnerable,
she growls.
Just when you back off,
she beckons you.
Just when you lunge for her,
she's gone.

*Just when you think you understand her,
she morphs into a whole new creature.*

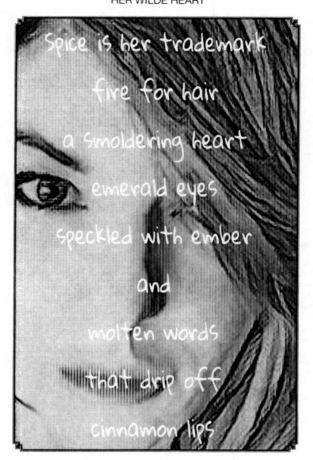

Spice is her trademark
fire for hair
a smoldering heart
emerald eyes
speckled with ember
and
molten words
that drip off
cinnamon lips

Bergamot and Ginger

She moves as enchanted mist
a scented trail of bergamot and vanilla in her wake.
Spice is her trademark-
from the warmth of her smoldering heart,
to emerald eyes speckled with ember
that singe with every glance,
and molten words that drip off cinnamon lips.

Royal Love

Your eyes a coronation;
they pronounce me Queen without a sound.
Your spirit, it decorates me in value.
We are an investiture of romance,
a regalia of royal love crowned in glory.
Our kingdom built by two.*

In reality three, for those who believe.

The FairReal Tale

You are fantasy and make believe
and the realest thing I've ever set my eyes on.

Fairytale Life

Once upon a life
you walked into mine
and it became the fairytale.

Read Eyes

If a picture paints a thousand words,
your eyes are a novel in the making.

Read Eyes Pt 2

Yours are a worthy read.
Those eyes are best sellers.
Cloaked in mystery,
I bookmark their perusal,
attempting to unravel their complex plot.
- A story I can't put down.

Your Name Alone...

I whispered your name across
my lips,
and it felt as though
I was shouting it from rooftops.

His Girl

She awakens the giant in him
yet helps calm the beast.

Spoiled

You chose never to love again,
then I came along;
sorry to spoil your plans.

No Habla Nada

We weren't lost in translation.
We easily and comfortably understood each other.
Words weren't necessary.

His Hands Speak

He is not a man of many words,
but his hands are full blown sentences.

Spilling Over

In the lounge of broken hearts
I observe the solemn faces attempting to appear unbothered.
In a corner, the defeated and forlorn,
wait their turn to express their
dark angst, which spills like drinks through their eyes.
They long to feel important. Some were once,
others never even given the chance.
Still they wait, as they get drowned out by the
noise of the self-absorbed doing shots and chasers,
acting beautiful at the bar.

The Edifice of My Now

Prickling skin awash with desire. Breathless childlike musings
brimming with red light-green light stealth (oh the strategy)
and the leaping of a hop-scotch heart.
Sweat to bone, song freed in gleeful yelp
of innocence and whisper.
Long before I met Whiskey and his meandering ways,
I drank to my fill of imagination with delightful inebriation,
sans hangover's regret.
Take me there, where we lived.
Not the place of hewn stone
not that of brick and mortar.
No, but the real one,
the place that built us.
Flesh and soil and blood that boils
which races and flows like rivers.
Where the earth shared it's secrets on side streets
of spotlight and mystery.
I would hide and you would eternally seek me.
Where laughter cracked the Summer night air.
Hand in hand in the land of forever falling Autumn leaves,
we ran to catch them desperately, joyfully falling ourselves
on cool grass.
Crisp breeze and shadowy bats fluttering above us.
We, lost in kisses and drunken wonder.
I can still smell the earth beneath me.
Lazy daddy long legs slept in webbed
corners as our spirits awoke.
Then is the edifice of my now.
Those yesteryears I will forever coddle as
entangled limbs for both the rush
and embedded discipline which feeds the
pleasure of this endless fire today.

What are you built from?

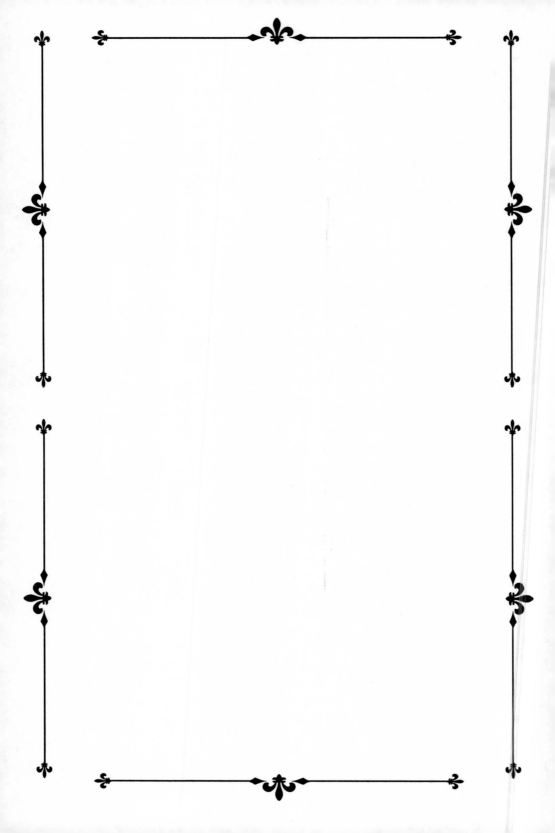

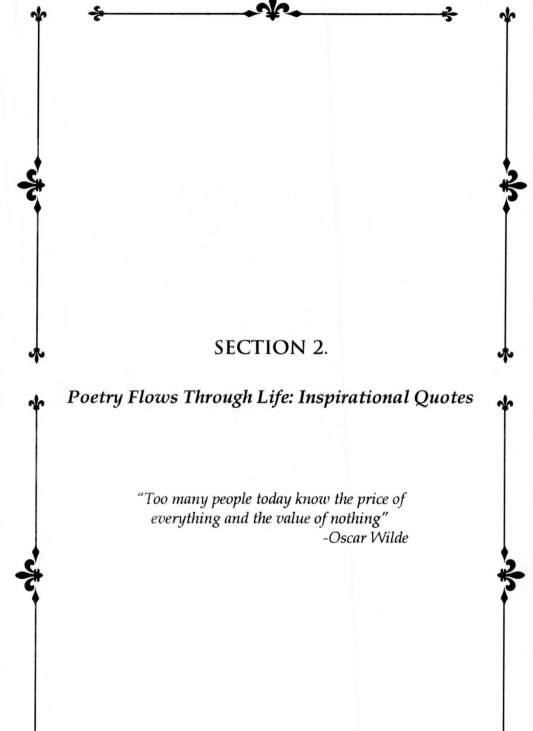

SECTION 2.

Poetry Flows Through Life: Inspirational Quotes

*"Too many people today know the price of
everything and the value of nothing"*
-Oscar Wilde

Respect her thorns
and the Rose
shall be yours

She is a Rose

Respect her thorns
and the Rose shall be yours

She is a Rose in all her glory.
Love her for her beauty.
Respect her for her thorns.

You are Exquisite

If you start to doubt your own exquisite beauty, Stop.
Tilt your head to the heavens. What do you see?
Is it not myriads of stars that twinkle so differently?
We do not deny any their awesomeness
even if one should flicker
or another shoot across the sky.
From constellations to morning stars,
all different, yet all mesmerize our minds and eyes.
And remind yourself, the brightest one
you may be seeing at that moment
may no longer be there at all.
So, lift your chin up you shining one.
In your own sparkling uniqueness, stand tall.

Not just to be read but acted on.
Believe it darling. Look up. You shine.

Gentle Warrior

An injured butterfly on the edge of a hurricane.
She may be delicate but frailty is no match
for her unremitting desire to fly.
A gentle warrior, weathering life in quiet victory.
What has beauty needs no sound.
Built by love, she shares sweet nectar with fellow wounded,
demonstrating how beautiful survivors can be.
Life flutters and brims even in the aftermath of a storm
because in her heart, hope is a healer, and restored love the cure.

Gentle Warrior

Injured butterfly on the edge of a hurricane.
You may be delicate but frailty is no match
for your unremitting desire to fly.
A gentle warrior, weathering life in quiet victory.
What has beauty needs no sound.
Built by love, you share sweet nectar with fellow wounded,
demonstrating how beautiful survivors can be.

Life flutters and brims even in the aftermath of a storm
because in your heart, hope is a healer,
and restored love the cure.

Courage despite hardship.
We can be strong even when broken. Helping others is key.
A strong but gentle heart where hope is worn as an amulet
and the relentless beauty to want to live our fullest
even when we are at our lowest, carries us through.

Take personal time to heal, but helping
others also helps us in the process.

The Motto

Use your Strengths to offset your Weaknesses.

This is one of my personal mottos that I live by.
I finally put it down on paper because I wanted to share what
has inspired me to reach beyond challenges many times,
beyond what I thought my physical limitations would permit.
I am not defined by the weakness. I am defined by how I deal with it.
Whether it be a health challenge, heartbreak, or loss.
Whatever you feel your weakness may be,
meditate on and find the strength
that offsets it. There is always at least one. I promise.
Is there a personal motto you live by that helps you get through?

Beauty Regimen: The Four Essentials

Beauty is an inside job

It is not only physical sustenance that we live on.
We must be fueled, formed, and maintained in other ways.
Emotionally.
Spiritually.
Mentally.
In our "internal beauty regimen", there are four main ingredients.
Each of these deserves our equal attention and respect.
They all need to be fed to support and thrive.
Don't neglect them or take them for granted.
You'll only be starving yourself.

Mind, Heart, Spirit, Flesh.

Princess Daughter

You are a beautiful creature of wonder.
Believe me, you will never be alone Princess.
Your endless dreams will always be right beside you.

Remember this always.

You Are Special

Nothing is ordinary when it is loved.

A Kind of Fashion

If kindness ever goes out of style,
I no longer wish to be in fashion.

Unstoppable

You cannot drown what lives in the deep
nor set fire to what already burns.

Be relentless.
Hands cannot choke a soul.
Bones that carry an eternal burn
can never be extinguished.

74

Dreams and Thunder

Her eyes betray her stillness;
behind them
dreams and thunder brew.

Silent Wars

Many a war is waged in outward silence,
inside the raging of the mind.

*You don't always have to announce or aggressively fight
for your goals, dreams, and strategies.
Let them feel by your quiet but constant energy,
that there is always something brewing.
Let your actions announce that in silence many a war is waged.*

Photo credit: Squigglyword

Wide Awake Dreams

Dreams aren't for those who sleep.

Don't fall asleep on your dreams.

The Burning

When you are partly made of fire,
turning up the heat is considered atmosphere,
and being consumed comes from within.

A little challenge is good.
And not always taking the easy way out
builds character. Thrive in the environment
outside your comfort zone.

Look Up

It's when I finally looked up to welcome the rain that
I noticed the rainbow.

*Hold your head high through every storm, and feel
the blessings along with the challenges.*

Envision

In my mind's eye, I envision a better place.
In my heart of hearts, I know I will live there someday.

What we hope for is what we find.

Tunnel Love

Be the light at the end of the tunnel in someone's life,
not an oncoming train.

Tunnel Vision

Sometimes the light at the end of the tunnel
is simply holding someone's
hand through the dark.

Silence is golden; a silent touch, platinum.

Love's Saving Power

Isn't to be loved
and to be saved,
one and the same?

Win/Win

True love seeks to win,
without keeping score.

HUGGING ON

A
long
silent
heartfelt
hug...
Is all I wanted to say.

Because sometimes there are no words.

Soul Kisses

There are kisses that quench a thirst.
There are kisses that leave you breathless.
Then there are those soul kisses,
those rare breeds of kiss,
that make you yearn.
They are light bulb moment kisses,
that leave you thirstier,
that make you realize how dehydrated you were.
They breathe life deep into you,
full breaths that resuscitate
what was once dying.
Deep
Core Reaching
Heart Wrenching
Mind Boggling
"Where am I?" moments of awakening,
where theories turn into living proof.
They linger
far beyond tingling lips
and stirred up ecstasy.
They are truth and purpose
that add life to your years
and bring purpose to your days,
and you wonder
how you even existed before them.

Seek the connections that really touch your life to be meaningful.
To build you. To give you meaning and purpose.

Meet Yourself

You really should like the person you hang
out with and talk to the most...
YOU.

Make introductions today.

F as in Faith

Faith it 'till you make it.
'Cause it's not fake that moves mountains.

Fake is a four letter word.
Fake can't see you through with any type of meaning.

Cut and Sow

We weave the fabric of our lives.
You decide which cloth you are cut from,
and how you will sow your character.
Let it suit you well.

Playing on the word sow/sew
causes a slight difference.

Can't Go Back

The trail of breadcrumbs always gets eaten by birds.
Don't you see?
There is no going back.

Move Forward.
Glance backward

86

Answers in Time

Time showed me things
no one else could.

Today Counts

Today will never return.
Make it a one of a kind.

*Whether on vacation, living your dream life
or waking up to a "typical Monday,"
every day is it's own day, special and unique.
Don't waste it!
Recondition your own mind to let go of the labels some slap on days,
like cheap propaganda.
Let's stop waiting for "Friyay" and Sunday
fun day" and stop dreading Mondays.
Let's realize that we are living, breathing, learning,
earning, yearning, deciding, growing every single
special and wonderful day that we breathe.
Do you have things to deal with? Deal.
Every day or moment does not have to be fun to count.
There is value in discipline and seriousness and struggle.
It builds endurance and character.
All of it counts and is special
because it is the only now you will get, never to return.
Every day you're alive is a gift.
Make the adjustment, feel it all
and enjoy whatever it is you will face today.*

Feel it. Here. Now. Go.

Don't Get Stuck

"Stop Hugging the cactus."
You'll just keep getting pricked.

I heard this in a sermon once and it "stuck" with me, pun intended*
But it is very worth repeating.
Let go and heal. Easier said than done, I know. But at least
start by thinking about letting go, let that thought enter
your mind, and start to back away slowly. You'll know
when you're ready to completely let go. No one should
ever push that, but at least know and believe you can.

*See Cheeky Section

Chalk Outline

Permanence?
We condition ourselves to read the writing on the wall
when most times it's just a chalkboard.

If it's killing you, change it! It doesn't happen overnight
and sometimes the hint of erased chalk remains, but it does happen.

*"Nowadays people know the price of
everything and the value of nothing"
- Oscar Wilde*

Photo credit: Krystal Candler

No Refunds No Returns

We spend time to buy money
in order to buy us a better time.
Alas, time spent can never
be bought back nor refunded,
not even a minute.
So think about how much
time money will cost you
and spend both wisely.

The Value and Cost of Real Thought

They say I'm a free thinker,
but I don't know-
It all comes at great cost.

Our thoughts cost us.
Every thought has a price connected to it.
Are you willing to pay for that thought?

Effort or Less

There exists an effortless
One-of-a-kind type of love
that's worth all the effort of finding.
Don't settle for less.

*You are worthy of knocking their socks off, not
having to prove yourself constantly.*

Longing

Desire has been manifested from antiquity.
Socrates argued postponing it to live.
Buddha philosophized eliminating it to live.
But, the heart that keeps urgently
whispering for desire and longing
validates that we *want*
to live.

Original Art

Nature's classroom taught me more than
any made of brick and mortar.
Art taught me to define nature on my own terms.
My terms turned brick and mortar into art.

Think outside the institution's box.
Deconstruct the box, make origami.

Question the Answers

With every answer I find,
three more questions take its place.

Give and Renew

I have never gotten weak from giving,
only from wanting.

The Blind Mind

I have never pitied the blind man,
only the one who couldn't see.

The Litmus Test

A lie can be believed,
rationalized, and even defended.
But, it will never be understood.

Test it.

Wellness Drug

Honesty,
the hardest little pill to swallow
and the one that makes you feel
most alive when you do.

Test It.

The Honest Truth

Being honest with yourself
surpasses being true to yourself.

Truth

There is no lie
in a look,
in a smile,
in a kiss.

Time Passage

Music: The most ingenious time machine
ever created.

Endless

Keep your imagination endless,
so you shall be.

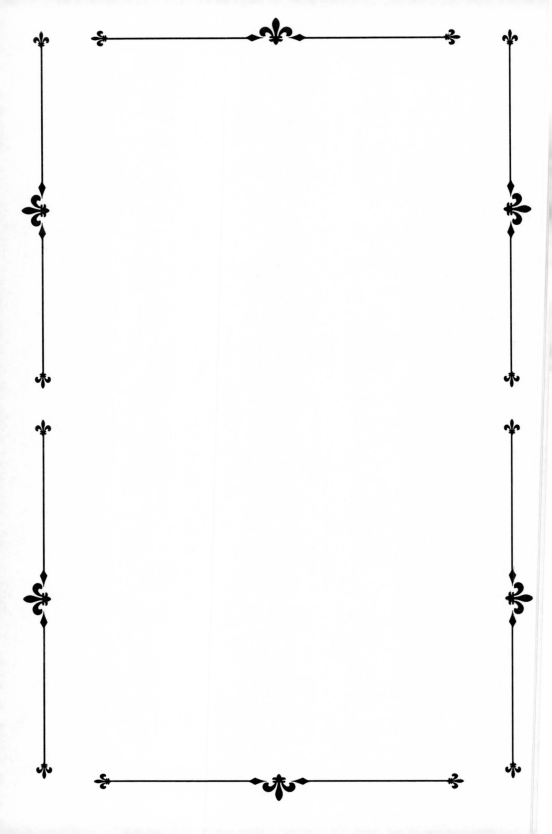

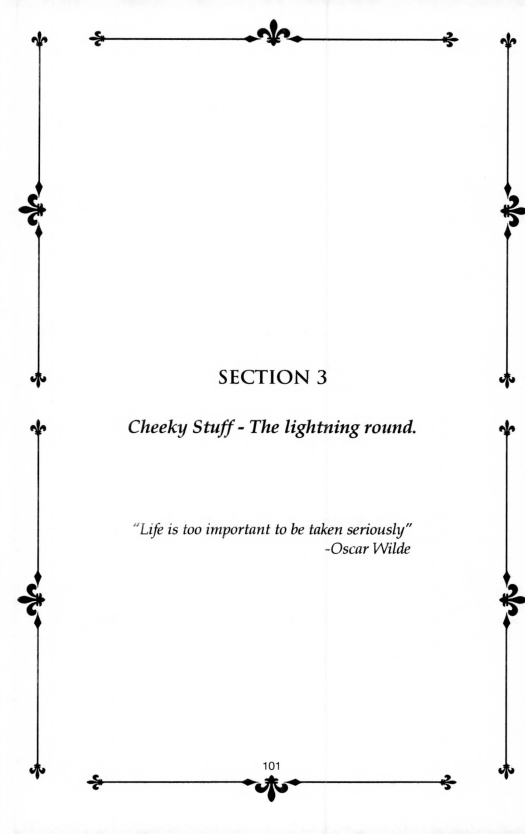

SECTION 3

Cheeky Stuff - The lightning round.

"Life is too important to be taken seriously"
-Oscar Wilde

101

Mosaic

I am a mosaic of everything
I have ever loved, hated,
or come in contact with
(without gloves).

No man, woman, or child, is an island.
We are all intrinsically woven in through and with each other.

Universal Negotiator

They say you can speak it into existence.
Now I'm in full blown negotiations with the universe.

"I have nothing to declare except my genius."
-Oscar Wilde

Scissors and Laces Untied

Some days running with scissors seems
to be the least of my problems.

Other days I run with scissors AND leave my shoes untied!*
'Cause I live on the edge.

*Don't try this, anywhere.

No! Pun intended

Puns should always be intended.

If you're that clever, you really should get credit.

Define "Normal"

I'd like to think
I'm normal
in a peculiar
insanely cute
watch your back
sorta way.

Loca Motive

She's a speeding bullet with a loca motive.

No Drama

I cannot play a role in your drama.
I am only contracted for romantic comedies.

No Fakeness Allowed

I do have a type: GENUINE
No Fakeness Allowed.

This is personal and the very core of who I am.

All In

I will match your wit,
and raise you a sarcasm.

Skinny B

If you want it sugarcoated try a powdered jelly doughnut.
Otherwise you've come to the wrong place.

Sugar is bad for you anyway.

No No's

Don't Tell me "No."
Don't ever tell me "No."
'Cause the opposite of "No" is "On."
If you tell me "No," It's On.

Moodyful & Limitless

I have no style
only moods.

Don't define me.

Timeless

I'll let you know about my midlife crisis when I get there.

Age does not define me. I define me.

Headdresses

I wear so many hats throughout the day,
halos, horns, crowns, and the occasional fedora.

A Work in Progress

Being a spitfire is not a talent nor is
anger a skill set.
I know this.
Yet still, I waiver.

Bitten and Ready

Once bitten, twice as ready.
('Cause I'm really not that shy.)

I bite back too.

Lip Service

Don't give me any lip.
'Cause I just might bite it.

Don't say I didn't warn you.

Telltale Sign

If we don't learn from our own story,
we are just chasing our own tales.

Joke's on You

If you take yourself too seriously,
you become a clown.

Then you'll have to join the circus.

The Effort

I will put my effort in making the best meal you've ever tasted,
not having to prove I'm worth going to dinner with.

Sighs Matter

Take care of her.
Sighs matter.

*"Oh, I don't think I would like to catch a sensible man.
I shouldn't know what to talk about."*
-Oscar Wilde

Hey Sparky

Those weren't sparks between us darling.
That was friction.

*When he thinks there's chemistry but
he's just rubbing you the wrong way.*

Mimbo

Oh yes, he's into his looks.
But, down deep,
he's very superficial.

'Cause we all know at least one.

Litto Morsel

You are deliciously clever,
and yummy to look at.

I love a clever mind and quick wit.
Make me laugh and I succumb.

Love Mustache

Got forever?
'Cause you do a body good.

Way better than milk.

Enoughest

You are more than enough.
You are enougher.
You are my enoughest.
That's enough.
I'll shut up.
Kiss me.

"It is a terrible thing for a man to find out suddenly that all his life he has been speaking nothing but the truth. Can you forgive me?"
-Oscar Wilde

Egos Sore

Where Egos dare to fly.
There, you Sore.

Keep Love Fresh

Is this love still good?
I'm not sure,
it's beginning to smell like ego.

Make sure ego doesn't spoil a good thing.

Smells Fishy

Be careful what you fish for
'cause you just might catch it.

Some of it stinks.
Be ready.

Speak Fresh

Some people speak and they are a breath of fresh air.
Others are just air pollution.

Please, Can

Those who can't, complain.
So, please...can.

Ugh

Don't be the pessimist who finds
the "ugh" in laughter.

Don't be that guy.

Assume...ugh

Partial knowledge is destructive.
Ignorance is not bliss.
And we all know how to break down "Assume."

'Nuff said.

The Wilde Ones

How brilliantly attractive,
the woman who can quote Oscar Wilde
rather than aspiring to be on Girls gone Wild.

"So let's knock a couple back and make some noise."
-Oscar Wilde

Drink Specials

Take me to your liter.

I drink because you whine.

How merlot can you go?

(These will be printed on shirts one day)

Don't Drink and Text

Drinking and Driving
Driving and Texting
Drinking and Texting

All equally stupid and dangerous.

An Ode to Freckles

A Redhead carries her sparkles with her.
Always the life of the party, she brings the confetti.
Her inner celebration pops through,
delightfully playing on her skin at all times.

Redhead Moments

A special dedication to Gingers.

Freckles loading...

If you haven't been called "Carrot Top"
by the age of eight, you are not a real redhead.

It only takes a redheaded minute to change my mind.

If you aren't able to tame a blond.
You certainly won't
be able to handle a redhead.

The devil too has an angel on one shoulder,
but a redhead on the other.

Don't mess with my family or friends.
It puts me in full on Redhead mode.

Don't make me go Redhead on you.
I've got it down to a science.

Blonds may have more fun.
But Redheads will burn a hole in your heart.

He said, "Be safe darling."
But, I live a Redhead life.

I am a Pheomelanin with an MC1 receptor.
(You know, a redhead)

Humble Final Words

Be I ever so humble,
there is no place like me.

"Live! Live the wonderful life that is in you!
Let nothing be lost upon you. Be always searching
for new sensations. Be afraid of nothing."
-Oscar Wilde

"My darling, continue to chase your hopes,
and never allow fear to catch you."
-Artemis

EPILOGUE

Dedication page

"The basis of optimism is sheer terror."
-Oscar Wilde

"According to Oscar Wilde, it is with sheer optimism that I take on every endeavor."
-Artemis

"This is history in the making,
a love affair for the ages,
a golden egg, with wings to fly.
I, I a mere passerby,
watching from the sidelines although in play.
Panting, waiting, in wonder and awe,
what will become of this.
It's about you and I.
Together we set this in motion or leave it still
dancing delightfully towards a beautiful future,
or leaving behind a bittersweet memory.
A once yearned passion.
What will be, will."
                                    -Artemis

Which will it be?
⌘

I want to thank my parents.
They raised a crazy non-stop singing, "had to express myself,"
little redheaded Greek girl. They not only
listened to me singing for hours on end,
they would make requests for more.
"How did you do it mom and dad???"
You are my hearts.
⌘

"I am her daughter.
I have her cheekbones and sass.
At her knee, I acquired strengths
and tenderness.
Through hand and heart
my mom handed her
many gifts
over to me freely.

Her love a precious commodity
that she bestowed to me in full.
I am my own woman today
because I am her daughter."

I am my mother's daughter.
I have her cheekbones and sass.
At her knee I acquired strengths.
Through hand and heart my mom
handed over her many gifts to me freely.
Her love a precious commodity
that she bestowed to me in full.
I am my own woman today
because I am her daughter.

I want to thank my love, my second hero, who
has continued to stir in me the desire
of self-expression and untiringly put up with the results.
You instilled in me the courage to take on this
incredible task of love and creativity.
This is for my father and you.

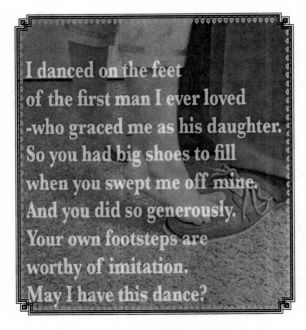

I danced on the feet
of the first man I ever loved
-who graced me as his daughter.
So you had big shoes to fill
when you swept me off mine.
And you did so generously.
Your own footsteps are
worthy of imitation.
May I have this dance?

"I danced on the feet of the first man I ever
loved (I was graced to be his daughter).
So, you had big shoes to fill when you swept me off of mine.
You did so generously.
Your own footsteps of love
are worthy of any man's imitation."

I am so grateful to Michelle for assisting with the
tedious job of editing, as well as to Eric, Isabel
and their team for their tireless work.

I want to thank Krystal Candler and Squigglyword for
their beautiful contribution of calligraphy to my words.
A very special thanks to the incredibly talented Joseph
Stevens Photography for his amazing work on my author's
photo and book cover. You're the best. I also have to give
a very special thank you to a little girl named Emma, who
danced on her daddy's shoes just for me. I love you.

Most of all, I want to express my deep gratitude to the
incredible readers, writers, authors, undying supporters,
and friends that I have come to know and that have
shown me so much love on this fun and fantastic journey.
I am thankful to you, more than you'll ever know.

These are the pieces you've chosen as your favorites,
so they are dedicated to you loved ones.
You are special.

"I didn't find you because I need you.
I found you because I needed us."
For Steven

"It's only when I became broken,
that I became complete.
For I have had the chance
to taste both victory and defeat."
For Michelle

"Beauty is an inside job."
For Rene

"Love me as if there are no tomorrows,
no yesterdays, and no what ifs."
For Leah

"From the cracks of her broken heart, new love grew."
For Lana

"Do the blues come in hues?
For, my heart exhausts
the color spectrum missing you.
Intensity hexed me.
O! Saturated ache.
Graying vision,
my world at the stake.
Silver lining tarnished.
Rose color glasses crushed underfoot.
'The blues' now rule.
They're sung and fueled
as I drag along in my faded suede shoes,
because we once had a royal love
that you forsook."
For Phillip

"You slowly undressed me.
You removed my sadness,
gently peeling off my defenses.
You stripped me of my fears
'til I stood bare before you.
What I once attempted to conceal as flawed,
you caressed and declared beautiful.
You called my scars 'trails of survival'.
Exposed, you witnessed the softness I once covered up so well,
looking at me in wonder,
while I just wondered why.
Then I saw it too,
from the image reflected in your eyes.

Now I wear a sleepy smile and tousled hair
as you wrap me in a blanket of your love.
Feeling like a true princess in how you adorn me.
I couldn't be more perfectly dressed
because your heart fits me to a tee."
For Lyle

❧❧❧

You never skipped a "like."

"We weren't in love.
We were on the fringes of passion, sidelined by fear."
For Rob

"Yours is a soul that has an open invitation
to visit mine, anytime day or night.
So, I will tuck my heart's key safely
into your ribcage.
Should you wish to call,
just let yourself in.
You know where to find me.
And know,
wherever you may be now,
you are always welcome here.
My love light will stay on for you-
Always."
For Geraldine

All photography and artwork is my own unless otherwise depicted and credited.

ABOUT THE AUTHOR

Ari has always had a passion for words and music. Nicknamed "Songbird" by her mother who also sang, is telling of her love for music, singing and creative expression. Bilingual and an avid reader from a young age, she has wonderful memories of conversations with her father discussing the etymology of words in both Greek and English.

She has been addicted to Scrabble, Words with Friends, and is a self-proclaimed Boggle Queen, with a deep love for enriching her vocabulary.

Her creative writing began in the third grade. Fueled by her teacher to pursue writing, she regularly won spelling bees, essay, and short story competitions. She started playing piano at the age of 16 and became involved in theater. Singing and songwriting were main passions until a tragic event in her life changed her ability to sing. Turning from piano keys to typewriter keys, she found renewed comfort and joy in her reignited love for the written word, her new voice.

She has deep love for people and community. She volunteers much of her time helping others improve their life skills and relationships. This is also reflected in her freelance work and writing. She is happily settled in her personal life and believes in God above all else, the first and foremost Artist and Poet.

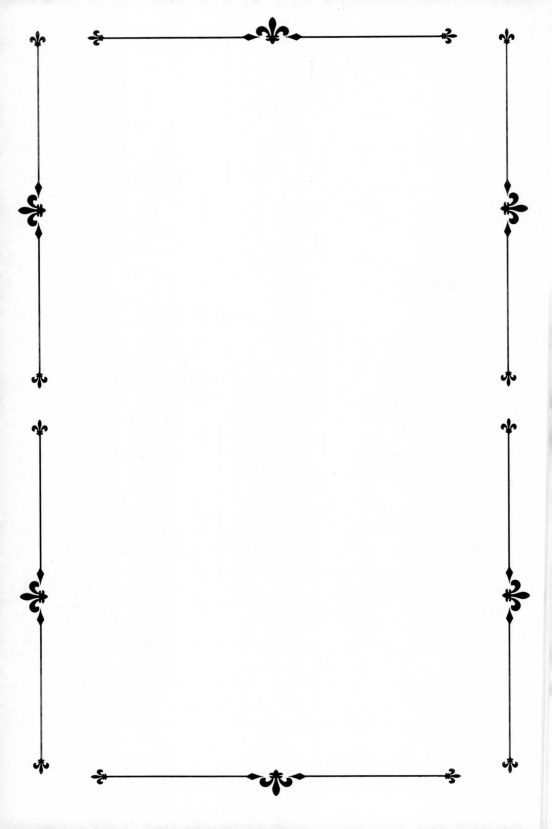